H
B
OUR
DEAD

ADVANCE PRAISE

Jonathan Travelstead maps the quest for his elemental "end points and beginnings." Doing so, he spans topography as various as Southern Illinois strip mines, automobile accident scenes, and Iraqi battle zones. What results are narratives that bare-knuckle gut-punch easy redemption. These poems honor the dead and the dying, refusing to avert the eye from certain explosion. It's no wonder the keenest offer "prayers" for hand tools that do something palpably useful, say, prying open the wrecked heart's flaming chariot of half-spoken desires.

—Kevin Stein, author of *Wrestling Li Po for the Remote*

Jonathan Travelstead's fearless poems are about the other in each of us, those sudden illuminations of the self in which we realize we are not alone. The voices of the estranged, the willfully forgotten, and the restless dead inhabit us. In any given moment, a lover's face or gesture reveals a mother we've run toward and away from all our lives. An electrocuted man's last minutes tick away to reveal our need to both connect with and hide from one another, to rely on comforting fictions to soften the truth, to insure that we don't go into that anonymous dark alone. It's a startling, affirming collection that stares down our other selves, compels them to speak.

—Scott Blackwood, author of *See How Small*

In *How We Bury Our Dead*, Travelstead sings out a tortuous and indelicate elegy that singes the most remote edges of loneliness. ...These poems escape and embrace the grief of his mother's death in equal measure.

—Travis Mossotti, author of *About the Dead* and *Field Study*

To Grandma - without whom & whose support this would not have been possible all my love,

3/13/15

HOW WE BURY OUR DEAD

poetry

JONATHAN TRAVELSTEAD

COBALT PRESS
Baltimore, MD

ISBN: 978-1-941462-07-2
Cover design by Rachel Wooley
Book design by Andrew Keating
Author photo taken by Charlie Nance

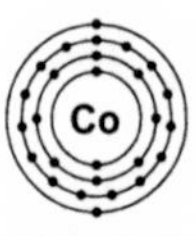

Cobalt Press
Baltimore, MD

cobaltreview.com/cobalt-press

For all inquiries, including requests for review materials, please contact cobalt@cobaltreview.com.

HOW WE BURY OUR DEAD

HOW WE BURY OUR DEAD

Part Three

Part Four

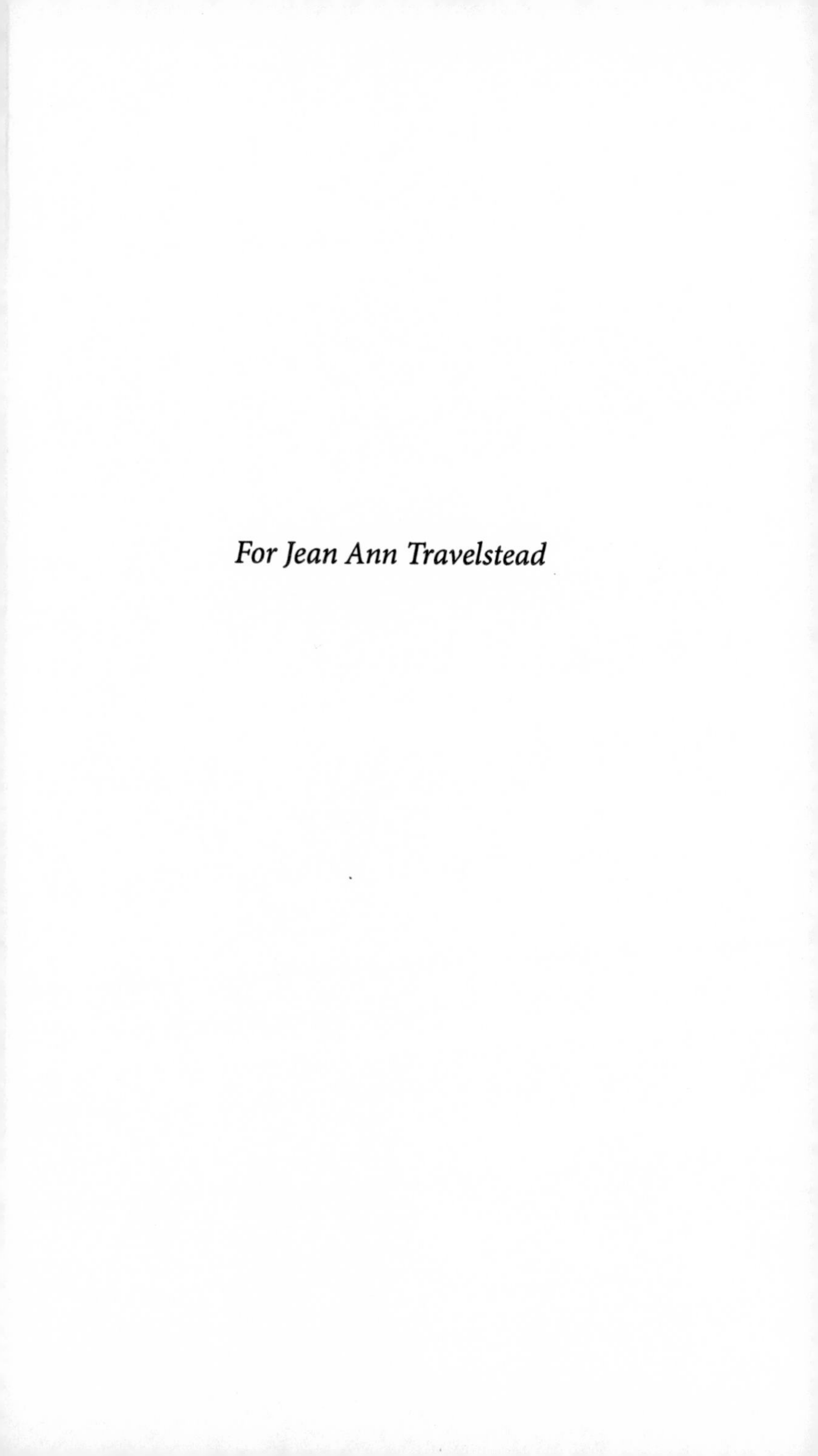

For Jean Ann Travelstead

HOW WE BURY OUR DEAD

Pawley's Island as a Portrait of My Mother's Dying

Today sunlight is a damp thing,
skin peeled back from scalloped waves.

The Atlantic bares its teeth
as tide cowers beneath mussel-scrimmed sand,
bits of fractured opal showing in the jawline.

From beneath the steel blue awning
we can hear the pier's timbers mewl with each heave
as the structure leans from light.

It is dusk. She won't see another summer.

When I shuffle her to the beach house,
even the sky's tired omens persist:

Signal flares flicker into light,
expose *V*'s of seagulls against the sky's drop-cloth.
They fizzle for a moment,

then snuff out like sparks in oil.

PART ONE

Pharmacological Dream of Travel Through Time and Space

I

So much to worry with the maths. The extra two hundred a month hazard pay volunteering for high-risk duty. At Scott Air Force Base, droning through ten hours of briefings and out-processing. Twenty-two hour flight. No sleep. Next to me, Fryman watching a movie on his laptop. Jack Nicholson is dying. Down twelve airplane bottles of Jim Beam—now forbidden to us—I count by the diminishing sum in one cargo pocket and the rising, empty lump in the other. Enough heart medication knicked from my grandmother's medicine cabinet to trip across the sky and back, but stilI I know exactly how long my mother has left to live.

II

Kuwait. We file out of the plane, filling a line of charter buses. Windows curtained with black felt, the buses hiss to a stop and we dribble onto the tarmac two by two. The captain yells and we form up. Tallest airmen front left, shortest, opposite rear. One duffel on our backs, another hoisted over the shoulder in a fireman's carry. Sand storms around us. Creases in our skin and the night sky fill with the base's alkaline light. Sober, I no longer trust my calculations. *How many seconds is eighteen weeks? Two bottles of Ambien. One hundred twenty Adderall.*

Captain America, Ali Al Saleem Airbase

Clanging fills the fire department gym
as Captain Lazzari hoists the forty-five-pound plates in pairs
onto the squat rack. Sweat beads his shaved, oiled head.
With each deep-seated repetition Lazzari chuffs at the air,

lets loose from his bowels a sonorous groan,
lunges upward, then sloughs his load onto the squat rack's
curved metal dowels he bends further with each slam of weight
against them. Airmen watch his poses between sets

like speculators admiring a stud bull that goes to auction,
or Michelangelo's David standing *contrapposto*.
Wrists together, pronate, Lazzari's right leg
jutted forward gives us a great view of the lineation

between muscle and brute will. Of Captain America
tattooed on his upper thigh—the hero's blue arm waving a charge
of green-fatigued GI's toward a face
flayed to the red skull of his comic book enemy.

When the PA clicks on and the tones drop
he's balls-deep to the floor beneath four hundred pounds.
The dispatcher's voice crackles through the gym.
A Humvee burns in a dune just off-base.

He pistons up, shedding the useless weight of steel,
and yanks his silver bunker pants over an erection
like a fist clenched around a roll of quarters
and burls outside where he clambers up, and onto the pumper.

En route towards the scene, base dispatch radios
the burning Humvee is cleared of soldiers,
and so they arrive to harmless slag—blown struts.
Riveted wheels bowed beneath a tanned, broke-axled hulk.

Nothing to save, "All Along the Watchtower"
bleats from the CD player jerry-rigged to the battery
through a hole in the firewall,
insisting there is no reason to get excited.

Still, Lazzari grabs a red hose line and blitzes
into the oily smoke of unidentified materials as if his skin
is galvanized, his lungs resistant as Nomex.
Fifty caliber rounds firecracker off at the Humvee's turret

and still he enters, swinging the hose—
charged, lithified with water at triple-digit pressure—
nozzle hoisted in bare hands above his gleaming skull.

Perimeter Run

What stone, what stoop, has not at least once
been spattered in blood? Saturday at oh six hundred
it is already a hundred degrees
when Lazzari and I drop our crumpled gallon jugs to the floor
and sputter off into an easy pace along eight miles of flightline.

Sand, punctuated by desert scrub
and occasional Doritos bags. We gauge our stride
counting breaths against the fifteen meters between beacons
and as we pass, a silver fox emerges
from a section of blasted concrete, trellised by rebar
as if to remind us of this place's history—
the busted-up bunker where unarmed Kuwaitis
were holed up by the Iraqis and while inside sketched
their last moments on the sloped interior walls.

One soldier in drab fatigues, helmet askew,
strap loose beneath his chin, drew his loved one's
hijab-veiled face—her potash, crescent eyes blazed in black
beneath the long, tapered sweeps and slashes of Arabic.

He wrote: *To those who discover our last stand*
give us glory when you tell of our siege,
then sketched a blackbird perched upside down
at a scimitar's downward point,
signifying how they fought, caged.

Picking up speed, we round the runway's end
and the red beacons there where the fox sits beneath the flagpole
where they hung the general,
looped the rope through the halyard and tied it
to the barrel of a T-55's cannon.
When they backed the tank it drew him up to the crown
and a soldier shot him through the head,
leaving in the pole a fifty-caliber hole big enough to sight in the moon.
Weary at six miles, we see a silver tail smear

behind the officer's mess where the remaining officials
marched under their own will outside
and lined up against the wall as the firing squad spat on the ground,
then chambered rounds into their Kalashnikovs.

Nothing is clean. Everywhere,
shallow grooves and thin lines cake with a dust
found in the pocked wall, stitched into brick.
We pick up speed for the last mile, sprint past the dining hall,
then the fuel depot, where I stumble,
see the fox flitting into its den as our footfalls,
then breaths, fall out of sync.

Hajji

The commander allows the Kuwaitis onto the base every fourth Saturday,
caravanning in their Isuzu pickups to the rear of the white prefab building.

Fathers in their white linens and *ghutrahs* rest on boxes and smoke
brown beadie cigarettes while their sons truck kitsch inside
they arrange on doilied card tables.

Before duty, I sit with *hajji* on a slat-board crate. He pinches a beadie
from the pocket of his *dishdasha*, holds it out to me.

As the sun gathers from its puddle of gas over the sand
we smoke and watch his youngest son thread in and out.

Sauntering around the corner of a nearby cargo container—then between us—
the angular stray cat airmen call 'Joe' curls against my leg,
and as I pet the feline between me and *hajji*, I am afraid for him.

I have seen video from a soldier's phone
of a cat lapping a poisoned sugar cube from a Kuwaiti's hand
who laughed off-screen as its body hitched and seized
then, raising his booted leg,
caved in its ribs there in the dusty street.

Even if I knew how, nothing I say could change a thing.

Hajji sees me, and I wonder if my sadness for what we call *animal* shows.

Hajji reaches his arm into the seat of his truck for a folded paper box,
untucks a flank of seasoned chicken
which he shreds to a cottony bulb on his knee,
then gathers it into his palm. Nods to Joe, then me.
Sprinkles it like gold dust into my hand.

Bazaar

One table is jeweled in Special Forces-style Pakistani knives—
black, light-sponging blades opened
with a thumb-flick. On another table, fake Rolexes
with Japanese gearings, neatly rowed and columned,
glass lenses tinted pale blue in their bezels

to resemble sapphire, identical watch bands anodized
in metallic colors. I wander through the clamor
and din of airmen and merchants haggling over cheap wares,
through the teeming crowd of desert fatigues and robes,
past a booth where handbags hang like carnival dolls

and the colors of a rainbow slinky jump from hand to hand.
Even as I push past cellophaned DVDs
with movies recorded last week by shaky camcorders,
ink bleeding through their photoshopped covers-
he calls after me. *Special price for you three for ten dollar!*

Then, desperate, *Four for ten! Cheaper than Wal-Mart!*
but he has nothing for me. He has no salve
for not being at her bedside.
Nothing hidden in the silver lozenges which contain Cuban cigars,
no hope that she will be there when I return.

But, there. I see it. The thing I can give her
in place of what I could not. On a shelf,
a red oil perfume dropper bottle, the glass stopper's neck
sandblasted for a seal. Holding it in my hands,
I see the gold leaf zagging around its perimeter

threatens to chip, but other than that it's perfect.
Better, even,
than the real thing.

To the Democratic Nominee. October, 2008

They broadcast on a delay so that no one will know you are here.
Secret agents in khakis file into the dining facility where today
the airmen get special treatment,
what *Food & Wine* says is your favorite meal:
Braised salmon and a ginger lime compote atop saffron rice.

Even as I sit, distraction finds me
in the royal blue napkin, gold-embroidered and tented
on the fine china, the Air Force symbol crested on its rim.
Along the left side three forks ascend in size
toward the platter—

Dazzled as I am by the decorum in the knife's burnished silver,
I miss your answers about foreign policy and the proactive measures
which must be taken so the U.S.
can once again lead the world in manufacturing.
It scrawls by on ticker tape I desperately want to end
until you wipe your fingers,
stand to meet me as if I am the special guest.

Your grip—soft like a woman's,
and your release—too delicate to believe, like a debutante
slipping off a velvet glove.

Struck as I am by the import of that moment
it is no wonder I give you a poem
I stayed up all night revising about a strip pit in Southern Illinois—
the poem that is not yet a poem
because in it as I move through the sick dimple of land
I focus on the way sunlight pales on fallen branches—
looking away from the scene
but failing to find again the leached clay or the dragline's bucket—
the human damage inflicted on that place.

We talk of writing and Saluki basketball,
if they will make the Sweet Sixteen again without Lowery—
and I also forget to ask if we can ever truly end an occupation,

or if you know that Halliburton and Kellogg,
Brown, and Root built this base with laborers
indentured from third world countries at forty dollars a week
digging trenches for CAT 5 cable.

Soon you will be President
but I want to tell you how many Bengals and Nepalese men
were killed so we could have internet—
red bandanas tied loosely around their heads—
now they are outside shoveling loose sand over their shoulders
as an Air Force sergeant texts his wife
when he should be watching the trench's boarded sides
for signs of breathing against the timbers
and for sand leaking from the compacted walls,
an indication they will collapse.

Yes, I know you must be going,
and you don't want the wrong people to know you are here,
but I should also tell you
that my father put through a call to me this morning,
to say that in her delirium my mother has called the police.
They're looking everywhere for me, but how can I help,
when I, too, am not where I should be?

Guardsmen. Ali Al Saleem, Kuwait

The megaphones click from the pole-tops
and what we call the Giant Voice buzzes *Fire Station One,*
respond to suspicious package at ECP Three.

Our sergeant packs into his baked potato suit
and onto the dusty pumper with the other foil-wrapped airmen.
En route, he refers to bomb threat procedures
in the red binder filled with indices and charts
listing minimum distance and manning,
apparatus placement, how many and what gauge lines
to pull if anything unfurls.

Because he is a high school physics teacher from Salt Lake
he has the books memorized on formulas and figures,
but has never felt an explosion's shockwave.

At Basra he saw his first IED.
Blasting cap in a cat's carcass,
nails super-glued to its matted, blood-napped fur,
det cord strung out its ass and across the street.

Last week the *pock pock* of Kalashnikov rounds.
Pirated M-16 tracers gashed the air, hissing into cinder-blocks
and powdering his upturned face
as he lay out at the makeshift pool, a red
heavy-duty tarp and PVC.

When the sergeant arrives
military police already have the *hajji* on his knees,
elbows flared behind his head at the cross-point between their carbines.

His pickup's bed is full of knock-off Louis Vuitton handbags,
blemished Ed Hardy jeans, and cigars in silver lozenges
he has been cleared to sell to airmen.
The black briefcase on the dropped tailgate?
He swears he's never seen it before.

Like Schrödinger's box,
it simultaneously *is* a bomb/*is not* a bomb.
We think both.

In the fire truck the sergeant fumbles his mic.
Stutters *Engine four on scene.*
Stages the pumper beneath two palm trees.
With a discharge of air the fire truck
sinks to its axles in sand fine as ground glass,
stuck, embedded there.

He doesn't remember
with the minuteman hose load you must step onto the sideboard
before taking a loop over the right shoulder
and stepping off.

Even I do not know the conversion rate.
Neither does Martinez, who, beside me in the other bucket seat
kisses his crucifix and touches his forehead, chest.
We don't know that a hundred meters
is still fifty feet short of the nozzle's reach.
Don't remember which lever on the pump panel to yank for foam.

Which line to pull: *bumper or crosslay?*

◆

It is still (*is not*) a bomb.
Now Explosive Ordinance Disposal parks their blue box truck
beside the fire truck at the perimeter's edge,
and the rear door opens like a roll-top desk.

The technician inside loves his miniature tank.
Has named it Number Five
after the robot in a movie from his childhood.
Its burnished, brushed aluminum body.

Its cameras and joints
he daily retrains from seconds to degrees
which he wipes and cleans with tear-open, sterilized cloths.

In the Quonset hut he has practiced for this day,
guiding its soft silicon tracks
through the labyrinth of white-painted curved lanes
and with a surgeon's unwavering hand, using its rubber-gummed pincers
to pull the egg from beneath concrete and rebar.

What is within reach—
Two orange cans of Rip It energy drink. A crinkled pack of cigarettes.
Two joysticks before a wall of monitors.

He whirs his baby on gray treads down the articulated, extended ramp
where Number Five trundles for the first time
out and into the world.
                                        After thirty yards,
severed from the radio umbilicus of its master
and last received signal, it makes a break past camel thorn and scrub brush,
past the kneeling prisoner and military police,
                              beyond the briefcase
(*bomb/not bomb*)

where it collides with the stone barricade and clatters to its side.

◆

Drab Humvees, tankers, and black Trailblazers line the perimeter.

Technicians lower a female bomb tech
into the green-pillowed armor built to withstand even the Kodiak bear.
Fragmentation. Heat. Overpressure.
                                                        Its weaknesses: Bombs.

Secured to loops at her side:
    tawny wire in fuses and coils, cubes of C-4.
Three colored skulls (yellow, red, black) dangling from a key ring,
a reminder of her civilian job as a mortician.

I know her.

Even in the suit, Vaverka's hips
are the upper swells of a funerary urn I once cradled
as she pulled out her pockets, taught me to kiss the rabbit between the ears.

Radio silence as she closes the Velcro blast flaps
and moonwalks over fine desert powder to the Samsonite case.
(*is/is not*)

Already I miss
her voice's percussive blast
when she called flanking movements at the training base,
marching airmen from the dorms to the adjoining classrooms
where I learned how to pinch a fire closed
and she learned how to dismantle a bomb.
How she taught me to go to my barracks each night
and tumble a handful of marbles in my mouth, clockwise,
until my tongue went numb,
the necessary exercise I had to learn
before finally triggering her body in my truck's bed.

I want her to say *Grasshopper* to me again
as we wake, the sun burning away Texas fog in layers.

I want her to tell me when it's ok to use my teeth.
But sweat streaks her Lexan faceplate
as she hunkers down in front of the case already sprung half-open
alongside one corner of which the leather has split,
exposed batting like cattail gone to seed.

In her armor she turns her face away, looks left over her shoulder.
Raises the lid, and I say goodbye to her delicate fingers.

Goodbye to her occupations with death.
Goodbye to her sandpaper vowels.

Rhanterium Epapposum

The *arfaj*'s taproot touches moisture,
slams from the cleft sand and drab, thorny bush,
each blossom a concussion against the sky.

Highway of Death

Before we leave the base, we undergo Cultural Sensitivity training,
then a bus ride to the Grand Mosque. But, instead of circling
the roundabout and returning to base, our Kuwaiti driver jags northbound
on Highway 80, where, sudden as white masses blooming

on an MRI scan of my mother's lungs I see what is left of retreating
Iraqi forces and Kuwaiti civilians trying to escape
in '91. Mercedes and Isuzus bulldozed off the shoulder
of the six lane highway, hunkered like black abscesses in rising sand

after B-52 stratofortresses and A-10 Warthogs disabled vehicles
in the front and rear, then mowed down everything between
in longer and lower sweeps until nothing moved. There she is,
my mother, in the duned tanks. Treads blasted off their tracks

in piles on the ground. In charred bus hulls and tractor trailers,
in the vinyl steering wheels where I still see the ghosts
of firebombed fingers. What grounds me is not the windshield melted away
to nothing, or empty space—a crater that concrete

and a Mercedes once occupied. The driver doubles back,
trolls by the wreckage again like a bird of prey making
another run, and like a mine it locates me: A bicycle's steel frame.
Rusted and mangled, rims scorched like the shadow flash

after detonation. It is this—my mother, clutching at me from every
busted war machine and crater, and now I'm cycling country roads
from what seems a lifetime ago. Slicing the air like a scalpel, chest heaving
as I tried outpacing the inevitable when she dropped a check

for five thousand dollars from her life insurance in my hand
and said any distance I ran wouldn't make her love me any less.
That's how I'm brought to face how I hide how lost and estranged
I am from my own grief that I think what I need most

is to volunteer for a tour in the Middle East, to be witness
to someone else's pain. A scrap of wind has finally finished tacking
a trek from her bed, across three thousand miles, to tell me
that in her morphine delirium she honestly believes

I'm still cycling those old roads. That same remnant of wind
also carries the names of roads where she thinks I might be found:
Thunderstorm, Chautauqua, Caraway Farm. Highway 80.
I let it blow through me, what paths I navigate home,

what fire pours around me.

Still-Life, Falling

Unexpected headwind,
and the olive drab C-130 screams,
nose down, into a dive.

Moon-eyed airmen awaken
floating above boxes
strapped to the fuselage floor.

The desert we return from,
the engine's burden and keening
no longer exist.

Everything I see is in suspension:
A combat boot, mid-tumble.
Aglet and lace, akimbo.

Globules of orange juice warble in zero g.

Narcotic snow, uncapped prescription bottle,
serene as Chinese pastoral.

The plane levels to flat air
and men rediscover movement.

Fingers, hands. Tongues.

Where endpoints and beginnings attach.

Martinez

Two weeks home, an email from the Commander. Martinez.
Police in San Juan found him filled with fourteen bullet holes, floating facedown,
knocking against a pier's waterlogged timbers.

I jog for hours, pounding my grief on Carbondale's sidewalks,
sweating it out, how we met as bunkmates—each sent from our home base.
The first night I heard him, muffled cries above me.

He saw it in my face the day after, in formation,
and I never saw his hump-knuckled sucker-punch, which came in low,
doubling me over and to the floor, though I was larger,

and he, easy to place in a cross-pin. Then he chopped at my ankles
and took me off my feet.
If I could tell him anything, it's that you never get the grace

of picking who it is you love.
That same dusty night we broke out the hooch he made from apple juice,
ketchup, and yeast rolls pocketed in his cargo pants,

stolen from the dining hall, and plunked in Gatorade bottles
that fermented in a slit cut in his mattress. We walked the base's sandy perimeter
in a parched ghost of light, bathed in orange,

chasing each slug of hooch with a red gummy bear as he told me
he sent his paychecks to his mother and three brothers without opening them.
It went this way the months we were there,

walking on the paved roads where our boot prints wouldn't give us away,
him telling me about his mother, who sewed clothes to support his brothers.
How a wrecking ball's overstrained cable snapped,

sent the ball plummeting to earth and whipped his father in half.
Joseph, I think of you often. How we throw our hurt
into each other like a fist, are confused enough to love what is not returned.

I'm still pounding it out, sweating my memories of you.
Hazardous materials training on the tarmac. Eight hours before
the next C-5 would touch down. It was a buck-twenty outside and you

were my partner in the simulated chlorine leak exercise.
Both of us in orange, airtight level A suits. Two layers between us
and clean air so, if your tank ran dry,

you would pass out before anyone got to you. I measured your entry vitals
on the clipboard and noted your anxiety in how many Pepsis
you drank that day, your hummingbird pulse.

I kept your claustrophobia secret. When we began our mission
to plug the punctured fifty-five gallon barrel, I was just getting the chains
to secure the overpack the moment you reared the mallet over the bung,

and your eyes rolled to the heavens, knees unbuckled, and when
you slipped to the ground my chest beat a hole no hands could fill.
I ripped the zipper down as if you were a breeched baby

suffocating in the womb. Your hot, dry skin. Rough as a cat's tongue,
slit open from the suit, I lay you out, flat on your back.
Ringed by at least twenty airmen, your eyes cracked open.

Smiling up at me, barely conscious, a thin stream of vomit
at the corner of your mouth. Clutching at words like maple seeds,
everyone learned your nickname for me.

Mother, you choked.

Mother.

PART TWO

Paper Lanterns

Daughter of a marine
sick, delirious for nearly two years,
you are the first woman I learned to fear.
The way you did your father's white glove treatments,
the man who threatened to give you away
for a smear of dust.

Your Saturday cleaning manias
as I folded hospital corners in clown sheets,
and made tight triptychs of bathroom towels
only ended in my pillowed crying because their edges
rarely aligned as perfectly as my welted calves.

Skinny-belted woman,
it is easier to remember your temper
as a sign you never wanted me.

Open palm stinging lines across my face
at a diner where, that once, I didn't hold open your door.
Thanksgiving. A bite of ham
struck from my mouth because my napkin lay, unused,
rolled on the table. Slapped at Cedar Grove Methodist
when saying the Lord's Prayer.
My head lacked the proper angle of respect.

I've carried resentment
for your puritan, southern discipline
like an ember in my belly,
smoldering, so that when I speak
potash rises in the air.

Today, I choose something better. A memory
of eighteen. Through the thin plaster
you heard me crying for the truck-driver's daughter,
the first in a string of women
it will take years learning I can't save from their fathers.

How you eased open my bedroom door,
laid beside me, traced letters of my name
into my back.

Hard woman
who saw children reflected only
in shined brass and porcelain,
how is it now that I slip toward thirty wishing
you could see me now, lilting Patsy Cline's
"You Belong To Me" as you pump
the Singer sewing machine up and down my torn jeans,
each note sparkling like glass fragments
brushed from my knees?

Mother, forgive me.
It took so long lancing the infection
I allowed grow inside me,
and now a sweet pain rises there
like the flickering eyes of paper lanterns
lit and carried away by the night.
Please forgive me for taking so long to know
I loved you even then.

Denali Star

The train out of Anchorage breaks down, freezes like a tongue
to the tracks. Everyone huddles

in the dining car arguing about Talkeetna. Where it is.
Whether we will reach the platform by dark.

The computer and the engine have stopped talking
and if it isn't thirty below then it feels like it.

There is no safe distance from a father and siblings
who take turns with her Ativan injections

as she points again to the hue of purple she wants on her casket.
In all this shaking of globes

to see where the silence settles, what else to do
but fall into a story where everyone stops pounding their fists

and demanding a time for arrival? Where you hear the engine
sigh to the computer: *Listen...*

This locomotive. This lonesome passenger.

Moose

Your earthy,
heaving tonnage before me
on the turnpike
is the riddle of an impasse.
A nimbus-glint above the blizzard—
the sundog's chimeric smear across sky.
You chuff breaths into vials
which disappear like belief in God
after unanswered prayers.
Your calf hidden behind you
tells me that soon
if nothing real comes between us
hunters from Cooper's Landing
will find me raked
across the Sterling's snow
and black spruce like an Inuit warning
against foreigners.
O Moose,
my heart beats
against the paper of my body.
You turn and continue
into the line of firs
so I name you Sufferance.
I name you Passage and Forgiveness
to a Cheechako's camo coat
and for a brief moment
I believe again the prayer
my mother recites
in her hospital bed
where an invisible Jesus
carries the speaker
over sand primordial as glass.
But, Moose.
No ghost carries me.
I hear wolves' moans slip
through the sky's ribs

and I know
you did me no favors.
I take back your names
like the temptation to myth,
a cold-blued hand
which seeks a glove.

Alaska

for JAT

Now let's say it's February and something else begins.
Your feet are only the memories of warmth, chiseled from blocks of ice
because you wear the wrong boots for this weather,
luggage lost on the last flight.

You are the three layers of clothes,
a roll of duct tape,
(gray *O*, mashed ellipse)
the headlamp in your pack.

The permafrost where black shows through to earth
and last season's leaf rot
spreads through winter like webbed glass.

The sky scrimmed by the Holgate's sapphire
holds you beneath it all—
It is easier to remain in motion than to stop.

Nothing in even the deadfall
you can point to and say is yours,
nothing you can say you are *of*.

At your right the Turnagain Arm,
a blasted still-life of the moon sleeving the ocean's inlet,
frozen rarefaction,
a neap tide caught naked in its physics
when the light gathers itself to leave. Stay.
A rumpled sheet pilled with fists.

A rifle crack of shifting ice sends your eyes
scurrying to the North where mountains like old men in sheets
loosen their capes.
An argyle cap with a man beneath it
pulls over his rusty Subaru
if only because he sees someone hefting a pack.

From your thermos, you slug down coffee
that tastes like motor oil,
                                        fumbling the door handle,
rehearsing your reasons as if they mattered.

Step back from interrogation and there is only this:
                              I'll give ya ride if you get right with dog,
a Pomeranian's tongue lapping your face.

Scenes from his landscape:
a son who discovered a love for figure-skating at your age,
a wife who carves reindeer from birch burl,
sells them on *the computer*;

His month spent each summer keeping fire watch
from numinous tops of giants—
with a shovel and the foil blanket that to need even once
means the firebreak failed and someone's going to die.

Listen, as he points at each peak you pass, says
that's my mountain.
                              And that one.

◆

And the Russian cabbie's Cossack, its oil-napped, patchy, rumpled mink,
  is probably nutria. And the inscrutable look upon his face
when, from the broken curb you hold out three crumpled bills
  like frozen flowers to him sitting in his filthy,

bottomed-out yellow cab. *Please take me to the hostel some girl*
  broke my English-degree bartender heart caught the first flight
to anywhere Gore-Tex gloves backpack lost
  on the connecting flight—words ghosting from the scared boy's

mouth in one steady, unpunctuated steam. Crisis recollected
  becomes the leap to absurdity. The sense of alienation, a comedy:
How, if the cigarette in the Russian's slack mouth falls, his beard
  will spark and burn like crumpled tissue, the spontaneous

conflagration of steel wool. The bit of home in your pack—the salmon-
  and green-colored cross your mother crocheted for you—
everything is days or inches from the body's need for warmth,
  so you think of George Clooney in a role he played

as a self-educated wandering hayseed when he said,
  this place is a geographical oddity—it's four days from everywhere,
how long you must wait for your gear, that, when it arrives
  fleeced of granola bars and the cross, the extra fifty

you kept for emergencies in the zippered pocket. It's then
  the gravity of the cabbie's gut overflows the steering wheel,
pulls *you* away to *I*, begins seizing like a pump gone dry, and you believe
  sure as Charlton Heston parted the Red Sea

that he's having a heart attack and you're suddenly on the cusp of self-definition
  and discovery, this strange moment of reaching forward
to open a crud-limed door, the entire scene sheened in expectation
  of a magical-approaching-sublime reward like the two-bit actor

who leaves the blonde whose legs never seem to end waving on the tarmac
  as his B-52 tilts into certain conflict the director makes
into a romance poster for the simple but highly profitable escape
  we make of war and travel, but it's a dirty trick and you didn't know it

but this tub of borscht barnacled to the torn bucket seat knows it
  and he digs deep in his stomach for something guttural to lob,
swipes the greasy-looking fur hat at your hand still holding the petals of money,
  peels away from the curb's black cinders.

◆

I can't help the feeling I've been in this city before,
where the sun hovers hours too long in a blunt lead sky.
The snow of Anchorage's downtown
is a bum's blanket cut into strips,
heaped in alleys, and in streets in front of bars with names
like The Kodiak, and Bear's Tooth Tavern (open till four a.m.),
a boarded-up gun shop with yellow post-it note
on the window that says *I am so lonely.*
It's light and I have no idea of the time.
The only person here
is a passing twenty-something brunette
on Third Avenue who looks familiar
in her black quilted goose down vest and fleece headband.
She sees me see her
trace a lock of jet-black hair over one ear,
then self-consciously looks down and to the left.
I call out a name that is not hers
but she follows instead a steaming torch—
coffee, held aloft in her mittened hands.
I know it would have been better
if this were a dream where the mouth
is clamped shut by the little brain.
Better not to puzzle
the correct sounds to pictures of thought
and cry like a wounded animal.
Better words remain without wings.
Better not to shake the bad rattle.

◆

Steel, diamond-plate steps rise into his big rig, into his world of flannel,
Old Spice cured into split vinyl seams and cracked upholstery,
the green glow of radios for light. His gorilla palm claps my shoulder
and I believe it when he Jake brakes twenty tons of chained snowplows
to a stop, says *That's what it sounds like to motorboat*

a fat woman's tits. Eighteen wheels of tractor-trailer unclasp
with an air horn blast, shocking the heart. Beating it back to life.
He's copied his favorite Robert Frost poems by hand onto a legal pad
and scotch-taped them to the crumbling headliner with every pine tree
air freshener he ever bought, each poem dated in red felt-tip.

I think of yellow-jackets and stingers, amphetamines. Vats of
burnt coffee swilled down the iced macadam, and when he says *It's cold*
as a fart in a dead Eskimo, it moves through my gut as true as this
landscape's breath. The doggerel he recites. Carnal. Kind as
the diesel's throb. Limericks of the North Slopes, clubbing seals,

rhyming the Alyeska pipeline with *you betcha*. Slushing past
the weigh station and the cop hidden there, a warning squelches too late
for salvation from his CB: *Watch out, Big Ben—wolf's in the chicken coop.*
My bones begin to hum, then resonate as the radio's copper-wound crystal
into the lambent night, and I feel like a pinpoint aperture

widening just enough to let this burly-shouldered, bearded light through,
a light once corporeal and distant as aurora borealis from the smell
of Illinois pollen. The truth is I can't remember exactly like it was
or what he said. Maybe it was that the Prudhoe Bay freezes hard enough
to cross in winter. Maybe that like the song that is always playing somewhere,

someone has to drive it all night long.

◆

In this lighthouse tavern are bell jars of moonshine
sweet as jalapeno rosewater. A black stovepipe
belches pine-knot plosives

into the timbers in such a way
it's easy to forget this isn't so much a place of warning
as it is a haven from ourselves.

Just in from offshore,
roustabouts in flannel line the bar, faces creased black
and sullen as they talk already of escaping

their women and children for the oil rig.
It is inevitable that the one who is drunkest among them
says *There's two kinds of people...*

but he is the one that's been rode hard
and put away wet, and I am the lucky oiled wick
which sputters to light—*suddenly*—

fatigued finally to the point of honesty
at hitching this icy landscape looking for a spot of green.
How amazing it is to admit

falling hopelessly out of love
with places where everyone is drunk, dangerous,
and armed with creeds at whiskeyed daylight,

to recognize these frigates of men
for what they are, as kamikazes who wreck themselves
against rims and icy rocks,

buoyed only by flickering mirages they make
against the walls of other shores.

◆

What does a boy tell from this?

In Alaska I remember the woman swerving to the shoulder. She has waitressed for years at a log cabin diner where the cook tells her to write out *no mayonnaise* above the burger on the ticket while the trucker tells her to hurry her skinny ass up with his over easy eggs.

She sops whiskey from her apron, asks the boy to drive,
and he feels the car-struts sigh, pot-bellied with their weight.

Splash of red, the rusted Toyota harries them each in their private
worries away from the Spruce's edge. Skids them back and forth
up mountain roads as snow falls in fat, white chunks.

The windshield wipers thud back and forth.

She sings "You Are My Sunshine" in a bright, clear alto,
falls asleep. Re-trued, he is a spoke upon the hub.

He feels like an oyster plucked and tumbled safely into a
burlap sack, the grit hardened within him to a pearl he has allowed
many to reach inside—each in their turn—and pried from his flesh.
These are the things he takes with him:

The lull of tires against wheel wells.

How it is that the poor care for the poor.

What takes him home is grace. What takes him home is the
sweet burden of strangers.

Aubade

In Clam Gulch ruddy face-rubbed doors

yawn open to frozen strangers.

Toyotas, Peterbilts, and Subarus—in them
the Samaritans' feet worry engines past all reason.

Hem. A gondola's *cree* up a mountain cable. Haw.
The low *burr* of tires grinding wheel wells.

◆

Dog, I know you by the sound of cloud-bit, over-mushed huskies
scraping time across macadam,

by airplanes and blackbirds which hover in the distance,
black-footed codas like the native's song
which wends its way above the rime

of Christmas tree, mountains, city.

—February, 2006

Fifty-Two Hertz

"Imagine roaming the world's largest ocean year after year alone, calling out with the regularity of a metronome and hearing no response... the animal is saying, 'I'm out here'... but nobody is phoning home."
—Andrew Revkin, *The New York Times*

Marine biologists listen
through their underwater instruments
to this solitary baleen whale
and name her for her song's
unique frequency,

an exhausted cry no other whales can hear.

◆

So we call her June,
give her a human name,
claim her as if we could erase her loneliness
the way we erase our own:

erecting antennae, slinging radio waves
like ships that sail beyond the script
on the map's border that reads
here be dragons,

hoping a postcard with a bit of code that says

You are

comes lobbing back to our wide, gray dishes.
Does not.

So we call ourselves billions
    of ones and zeroes
exiting a hole,
falling from a scarp's blasted entrance
to slate-bruised knees
                    where we pray for a story
we can believe.

◆

Or we pray for rain to fall as snakes
        that bite their tails in prairie grass
and roll to the horizon

        where dust-browned leaves rise in a conjured gale.

Or we pray for tufts of nebulae
        that shake glimmering dust from their locks,
christen our foreheads with soot.

Holding out for a switch flicked in the heavens,
we pray for confirmation.

◆

June, what if your song returns from a distant place?

◆

An alien haunted my bedside as a child.
Its almond head,
the ink-black ovals that passed for its eyes
paralyzed
me in them,
one brackwater finger
held to its subtraction sign mouth
took from me the knowledge I was alone.

◆

June, let us each come forward
and join the swelling solitudes.
Let us commune
in this dark's first burning breath
and experience
the stars' frequencies,
individual in light and sound,

each unique as the fingerprint's gentle sine

shining their celestial voices down on us.
May we not refuse their beauty
which says
I see you. I name you.

PART THREE

How We Bury Our Dead

Nine-thirty a.m., Thursday, June twenty-seventh.
My parents' home. So who are these penguin men who take
the wash cloth and plastic tub, the dropper
of absinthe-tinged morphine from my father's enormous hands?

The funeral men have come, though no one remembers
who it is that called them. They soothe my sisters, myself, and brother
in succession, hands guiding our shoulders
to the sunflower curtains of the kitchen.

Narcotic blue pooled in the sink's chipped porcelain.
Coffee, cold and still in its pot. Because we have paid them
to dictate for us our farewells,
they take special care to assure us that bathing the body

is no way to milk pain from the hands,
that we only increase our trauma with each stroke of my mother's slack,
cooling cheek. Stitched together like a quilt.
This is how they coach us to wait, to save it for the reenaction

in their Victorian rooms of veneered particle board
and crushed velvet as if the pulse could rekindle for bad taste.
Scene. Tie snared around my neck.
Blurred queue of faces and run-on condolences

parade by the body I now only remember with exes for eyes.
Where is the comfort where nothing is understood?
Where, in the twenty-third Psalm's pastures and valley of death
do we begin forgetting how it was

that when we were apes and said goodbye
we gathered around what is lifeless with low hoots,
hairy fists just uncurling from anger at the sky
before dragging the cicada wings of our hearts into the reeds?

We forget, too, the cloyed smell of rose petals and orange peel
means ghost, that a host of sparrows
ferry the body's remainder across the river—
the body which was once packed on the dining room table with rosemary

and lavender by the son so the family may then begin
lowering the weight. What I feel instead is an anger
they tell me is impotent, worthless. An anger
they say I don't want and should not feel and so it returns to me

and returns to me. It comes as grief that gloves the tongue,
dulling a taste for sweets. It comes like a rag-tipped phantom, lingering
at the corner of sight in July's baked afternoon,
and it comes like an opiate. Making each lover my mother,

it comes as I find sex joyless and strange because, by opening the box
where they placed a scarecrow that almost looks like her,
I forget that warmth leaving my palm is what means *goodbye.*
Ask yourself who buries *your* dead? Go on. Not you.

Garbage men paid with a discrete check in the mail.
George & Lenny with a backhoe and spade in a crude American Gothic
for *Funeral Times* magazine, dangling cigarettes in the only hole
that separates them from making rent

and two cases of beer a week as they talk about that patch of America
they're gonna call their own. And all those rabbits.
This is how you look away.
This is how we bury our dead.

PRAYER OF THE K-12

Lord, let me start with one pull,
my bar shuddering in your calloused hand
as you ratchet my disc
to the scream that melts cast iron.
I pass through it, a ghost through rebar.
Chattery teeth, set on the floor and released.
On a house of cards, a tidal wave.
So much you have engineered, Lord.
I beg you let loose my chain
so with my carbide teeth
I can chew through the paper of this world.
My god! let me do what you made me to do,
and growl beneath your trigger finger.
Let me tear this place in two.

DuPont Paint Factory

Two officers have located the victim in the abandoned
building where the copper-thief says his friend is on fire.

He said they scaled the barbed wire fence topless,
one at a time, t-shirts wound around their hands for the spikes.
He said he doesn't remember trying to wrench his friend loose,
how he got the hole blasted in his hand,
or the twenty minutes it took him to limp two miles
to Saint Joe's Hospital.

We cut the sirens, leave the lights warbling
across the cracked red brick when we hiss to a stop.
Use bolt-cutters on the chained gate,
park Engine Eleven at the rear of the building,
use the K-12 to slice the hinges of the heavy steel door
I help Jack slide from its jamb, and lay flat on the ground.

The officers are already inside,
have heaved themselves through the thieves' entrance,
the busted window. The cherry of Tate's cigarette
appears before he does in the dark doorway,
nodding in the direction where Bearden—
Samantha, a friend I call Sam—waits with the victim,
crooning to him *it's gonna be alright, champ,*
help is coming, help is here.

Entering the cavernous room,
I can smell it for the first time the way I always will
(here on out forever and forever amen)
the first few moments of each time the tones drop
in the middle of the night—
rancid meat, bone's charred powder,
fear in a bundle of thick-wristed copper wires.

I'm close enough to count
how many breaths Jack takes in a minute,
close enough that if I reached out
I would brush the thick material of his turnouts,
but not nearly close enough to say aloud
that sometimes it is good to fear what isn't seen,
or good to fear what isn't understood.

Shattered windows crunch beneath our boots
as we move slowly forward, slicing the tight beams
of our LED flashlights
through thin layers of smoke and the voltaic dark
where first human—then robot—arms once stamped
lids onto one-gallon cans streaming by
on black conveyor belts.

Sweat is a cold layer of rubber coating my body.
I hear a whine like the yipping of a trapped coyote
and think an animal has made this place its home.
But then I realize in the center of the room, a substation,
inside it, whoever is stuck, still alive. Crying.

Sam, talking softly where she points her flashlight,
then turns to us. *Thirty minutes*, she says.
Thirty minutes electricity has been churning through him,
leaving a blackened trail like wildfire behind it.

Sam tells us do something, *please...*
then goes outside and props herself by one arm against a light pole,
pukes in the rain as Tate wicks another cigarette
into his lungs and pats her back, chuckling,
then goes over the digital pictures he took for evidence.

The substation is boxed in sheet metal
and an insulated column rises from it like a chimney to the ceiling.
I can see the panel which has been removed
at chest height and placed on the concrete floor.
The neon warning, stenciled on it in blue spray-paint:

DO NOT TOUCH!
ENERGIZED, MARCH 2010

Jack says relax, it's too late, his insides are blasted,
there's nothing we can do. Jack says go ahead and look,
go ahead, I've seen it all before.
Jack says...

But I don't feel whatever it is
that mutes the urgency in his blood so he can lean back
against a wall, one boot crossed over the other
waiting for the lucky guy who's next
on the power company's OT list to arrive
and shut it off at the transformer,
then go home and back to bed.

Inching up to the opening,
I see the back of his head and the silver chain
which has blackened and sunk into his neck's flesh.
I can tell he is still alive by his moans
and by the hum of voltage and by the way smoke dances
above his body, naked and fetal.
His clothes have burnt away to only his collar and a thin strip
of denim around his waist.
As he climbed inside
he must have brushed the copper cable thick as my wrist
elbowing down from the shutoff switch,
that, without any room to get away, must have held him down
against the concrete floor, against the sheet metal walls,
making him and the substation both part of the circuit
as it passed current through his body.

It's a blessing he's stopped moving.
Thank God, it's a blessing we're here to help.
It's a voiceover.
An act-out of a joke we don't laugh at,
and if we do it comes out bitter and mean
because I know we have done all that can be done
for a body that has been wracked by electricity—

                how it enters and branches through
what is sixty percent water, cooking the blood and muscle
   and bone as it arcs from cell to cell
                     until it blossoms out like a hollow-point round.

And what could we have done?
Not climb inside and pry him from the cable
with our fiberglass pike poles.
Not remove another panel because if he's leaning against one
he's leaning against them all.

I feel burned out and hollow but can't look away.
It has been twenty minutes since he has moved,
at least fifty since being electrified.

There is not one, but two, exit holes.
Smoke ribbons from a hole in his stomach
and the blasted joint where his elbow should be.
His eyes drip from their pinched lids like egg white
and belly fat has melted and run in stringy
yellow-brown columns to the floor.

Then I see his shoulders rise and fall.
Hear a low-throated moan that sounds like rip-starting a chainsaw
and know it can only be a death rattle.
And though I don't know how he is still alive,
Jack and I give him what we can.

We say *We're right here buddy*
we're doing everything we can buddy
what's your name
we're gonna get you out of here real soon
can you say anything buddy?

Hard to accept that even when what you say is true
what they hear is the lie your heart hides behind.
Hard to accept when his breathing finally stops
and the end looks like a second chance,
that this is how some of us go—
naked, and black, and boiled in our blood
while those supposed to save us only stand by,
always waiting for someone else.

What else can I do but look at the place
where the leather of my left glove has come unraveled
from hefting the axe too many times this year.
What can I do but fix my eyes on the unraveling seam
I swear to god I'll fix tomorrow,
though whether it will actually hold I can't say.
A lyric from a song ruins its way
through my head and I take my place next to Jack,
help him hold the wall up.
I ask him if he's heard the one about the meth head
who breaks into an abandoned paint factory.
He says yeah, but tell it to me again.

Prayer of the Maul

Let me sweep aside a factory wall, Lord,
cinder-blocks preventing passage
to an engine room scrolled in flame.
I am the grunt before thought.
My load is greater than your stamina,
and though I am your simplest machine
if you let yourself love too much
what is inside the mountain
I am sure to burst your colossal heart.
Even in my dreams
I am a juggernaut ready to destroy all things.
I pray only that you heft me
from that place between your shoulders.
Let me be the one chosen.

Shock

He turns off his cell, stays home Saturday night.
Sits on his living room floor,
arranging empty bottles of Stag between his legs
as he watches John Goodman play a shell-shocked Vietnam veteran
who pulls a gun on his friend in a bowling alley.

There may be a full moon outside.
A vague notion he is supposed to meet a blonde downtown.
If someone knocks he doesn't notice.

When he clips the jag on his fingernail
that pierced the latex glove he used in the paint factory last night,
the sound of the movie is replaced by the wet paint sound
of the body as it peeled from concrete.
His ellipse of cuticle
is the brown skin and marbled strip of fat left behind,
fused to the galvanized steel grating like burnt meat on the grill rack
and now the paramedic is telling him again
to grab the legs and help him lift the body into the bag,
and he no more than clasps the charred calves
when the meat slips off the bone,
exposing the tibia's pink and purple ball.

That moment, frozen—
as it slides like a greased marble along his bare wrist
between his cuff and the glove.

He smells it under the piss and ink odor of beer.
Lifting the spot where burnt flesh touched his wrist—
the smell of cooked meat is imprinted there
like the throbbing pain left long after a limb has been lost.

And just like the game of mouse trap
where the marble has already been put in motion,
he can do nothing to stop the thoughts' tumble toward climax,
that the boy's body smelled like the pork shoulder

he and his partner from the station barbecued at the Fire Department picnic
on Labor Day for their families as they gathered at Riverside park.

That like the symbolic body of Christ
taken beneath the tongue in Mass, dissolving to a paste
so his body can better become yours

their wives and children ate the body
and they gave scraps to the yellow Labrador
that Captain Tripp's daughter stumbled over
as she played badminton and they clinked bottles together
while the blues band played,
eating until a pain filled their bellies.

He can do nothing to stop the slipping
rack and pinion of his mind,
how it was nothing so unpleasant as the rancid char of those
he has found crumpled at a door or window,
dead from smoke inhalation but only a few feet from air.

How he's starving, but cannot eat
not because of what persists on his hands or the fabric
of his turnouts
but what he can't wash from his mind.

This is the job that chose him.
The one where no mask seals tightly enough
against the face so that you will never have to taste
what circles a worn track
deeper in the mind,
a memory that is named *Danger*
that sniffs and gouges its snout where it will sleep in its ruin,
turning no cure to the light.

Therapy

The woman I'm seeing off and on, two years on depression meds, without work.
My neighbor, fifty and bald from chemo I sit with mornings,
drinking coffee as she pets my dog.

I think *This time I will be there.*
This time she will live.

The therapist leans forward, eyes cresting the silver rims of his glasses.
You can't really save anyone, you know.

Shame like water rushes into me, fills me like cotton-jacketed hose.

Nothing to say, I look at the book on the coffee table
for what must be the appropriate amount of time.
Then the gold clock, its ticking encased in glass on the desk,
three spheres spinning on its mirrored base.

Good, the therapist says, leaning back. *Good.*

◆

Why can't I tell my father about the electrocuted boy?

Try. Talk to him now, pretend he's in that chair.

My father, a spreading wingspan of a man
named after a Ford and a character in Shakespeare
who herniated a disc and the meniscus in both knees
working doubles for UPS so we could go to the beach each year.

Sleeping beside him for a week of nights
in the shallow dent my mother's body left,
each time our backs touched his breath threatened to not return.

A story. It comes to me from a life ago. Bible School. Of Ham,
who, finding Noah drunk and asleep, covered his nakedness,
and how when Noah awoke, he woke ashamed
and cursed his son for seeing him in his human weakness.

Tell me how can I come to him for comfort
when it wasn't the electrocuted boy I saw there but myself,
helpless to his own singing grasp
and clutching the copper cable like the third rail of life?
Tell me how I can be anyone other than I am,
please—how when not the least part of me
leaks beyond my father's pooled shadow
that I can now go to him with my smallest of pains?

With this crumb a stronger man could pinch in two.
This infinite fleck of nothing, this small worry.

Prayer of the Wild Hose

Lord,
beneath your load
I break these brass bonds.
A gas-filled house has exploded,
and under a pressure which is too great
my cotton jacket's blasted ends rise to meet you.
How clearly I see
all that is couched in the tops of trees.
Clothes, knotted and black.
A doll's arm, its socket.
Scorched chicken feathers.
How true it is
that every cry whisps to vapor
even as I spin and whirl,
spouting, a cut snake.
This, is it Your construction?
These, Your children, sleeved in darkness
as you stopper the bottoms of doors with cheesecloth
and shear the copper pipe?
I see You flickering there in the alley—
You want blind adoration?
Then crawl toward me on your knees
without the black helmet.
Try wresting my ragged, whipping ends
back to the ground.
Take from me what you demand
and go.

Prayer of the Flat Head Axe

Lord, let my wide blade
part the roof's shingles and plywood
from the red sea that roils beneath.
Let it find burl,
the sweet spot where timber shudders
and splits at a single measured blow.
I am yours to command.
I will not spark or chip on hardened steel.
My yellow shaft
will not hum the impact to your arm.
With the same smoked hands
that carry me into char
please wash and hone
my edge again. With oil,
anoint my head as your only child.
I pray that no one need entry
or a path hewn tonight,
but if you will it, Lord,
let me be the tool.

Separation

This is what numbs it.
Coming in early. Empty station.
Filling out the time card. Morning walk-around.
For the first time it feels like a job.
Starting the fire truck's engine. Dialing up the pump.
Hoping the diesel's rock and rumble
will for a scrap of moment take his mind
from the kitchen door,
how it hung in the amber cast of morning,
the slash of light coiled on the bedroom floor.

That he could forget the empty house,
and the unfulfilled promises. Forget the spot,
bald of shingles. Vinyl siding,
missing from the last storm.
That he would see someone, have work done.
Solve anger with Wellbutrin.
No more strip bars.
Budget. Take her out once a month.

With a clipboard
he inventories the compartments for his imperfections.
Tines of fog nozzles, that they are not missing. Check.
Screws tight in the mounting brackets. Check.
Hoses, insuring that the couplings' threads
have not faded from repetitive fastening.
Indications they will fail.

He clatters through boxes of fittings,
searching for what is missing.
But no box on the sheet exists he can slash,
saying *she has come back she forgives me*,
so he flicks the siren, clicks the mic, toggles the light master
until he finds it. There it is—
In the bubble flasher a light that does not turn.
His heart is a sewing machine

as he climbs up onto the truck's cab. He winces,
hearing the sharp sound of plastic breaking—
the red housing, as he yanks it from its screwed base.
Inspects the bulbs, finds the filament and ballast intact,
but failure is the focal point of this religion,
so he traces the wire's lead
through a hole sealed down into the cab
and does not hear the mechanical trundle
of the rising bay door, or the Chief as he enters,
or the Chief shouting to stop,
so busy is he slicing away at the headliner
with a utility knife, and pulling out fistfuls of batting.

Cellulose snows down
in the sunlight plunging through the open bay doors.
It's hard to watch—the tourniquet,
tight around his chest. The short in his life
that seems just beyond reach.
A man who dismantles his left hand with the right,
the truck's insulation continuing to fall against
but never *through* a man
too blind to know he's on fire.

Prayer of the Halligan Tool

Lord, if anyone is trapped,
let the point of my crow's bill taper enough
that I only need tap
and the car window powders
like snow to the ground.
Let me pierce, then fold back the hood
like crepe paper
to cut the battery's red—then black—wire.
My flat bill is yours. My body.
Your finger and thumb
spread the door from its crumpled frame
to the blood-webbed and shocked—
a pinned woman begging forgiveness.
Lord, when your chest hitches into your throat
let my curved fork lever the burden.
Let me bear the weight.

Dream of Car Wreck and Failed Extrication

No *thwock* of ignition, no *whump* of heat sails by
as I squeal to a stop the cardboard box.

Glass powders the highway like snow.

Strobes churn the dark. My ego radios for help
as I rush pell-mell with a dull axe
                                        and the Halligan's crow-billed
steel fork and spike
towards the crumpled sedan melting in front of me.

Now the car is a dogwood flower that's sprouted pink,
                        sudden and enormous from the broken yellow line.
Petals swollen, salmon glow
flickering against a body trembling inside.

                                                    Always the wrong tools,
my set of irons clatter to the ground, my hide-thick gloves.

My fingers trace clefts until the folds part
and unfurl to asphalt,
allow entrance to the cindered body inside.

I touch her blistered lips with mine.
I knew her.

Because no one is coming
I plunge the crackle and rind of her chest,
snapping ribs like kindling,
reaching the cavities of her heart,
                                        which I cup with both hands

as if with the right touch the pump will start again,
her eyes open like I remember,
and this time she will love me.

Ralphie

You call the station every night at seven.
You call like an eight year old though you are seventy.
You call because you still love John Deere tractors
  and red fire trucks, and Nancy taking you to Amtrak
  on Sundays just to watch the trains go by.

Cornfield baseball in October after the crop's brought in.

When you call you ask
  Who drives the engine if there's a fire today?

You ask
  Who opened the big doors this morning?
  Who will close them tomorrow? you ask.

Always the same questions when you call.

Lincoln Logs in the driveway.
  You didn't hear your mother
  and remember only the finned tail lights,
  but your head ponged off the bumper,
  and like a scrap of light your mind travelled hopelessly
  from that moment on in a straight line.

You call because you want to feel safe.
You call because you want to talk to God.
You call because you think we know something.

We've hung our coats from the chrome discharges and intakes.
  From silver rails and the feet of ladders.
We've cooked and washed the dishes.
We've showered, and turned off the news
  because at seven we know you call.

And you ask: *What did you have for dinner tonight?*
What did Wildman fix for dinner tonight, yeah?
And we say *fifty hot dogs, Ralph. We're gonna beat Kobayashi this year.*
And because it's not bad teasing if you laugh
we say beef and *noo-noos* when you call.

Ralphie,

Through long nights spent chasing fire through the void spaces, through short ones with none at all—everything that burns seeming to wink on and off with no pattern, you are a pigeon released in the mountains that somehow returns home. The one thing on our shift that doesn't change, we know what you're going to say before you do.

Ask your litany of questions.
We will answer when you call.

PART FOUR

Prayer of the Motorcycle

> *"I tell you," he replied, "If the disciples*
> *keep quiet, the stones will cry out" —Luke 19:40*

Lord, cover my machined skeleton
with soft muscle rippling beneath skin.
Trade me an irregular beat
for the perfect timing in my finned chambers.
Powder-coated steel. Ninety-two octane.
I too am a collection of precious dirts
plucked, fashioned from the earth's heartbox.
I need sweet air, fluids. Spark. A master.
Give me hunger
beyond the bite into a curve's pavement.
Lord, give me sight where I have a filament.
If I am their creation, I am yours,
so give me the freedom of a misfiring voice
and the tiny loping engines of cells
whose fuel is bread, meat.
Then let me ascend your highway
with the sputter of wings.

Mitch's Motorcycle Salvage and Rebuild

I push my Suzuki by the fading red-and-white-striped pole
and jangle through the front door of the repurposed barber shop,
where, in place of combs pickled in jars

of green sterilant and leather strops, and slender razors that unfold
from pearled black handles I see instead the butt-filled piston heads
of old dirt bikes like hollowed-out ends of leg bones,

and a long, mirrored wall oiled with posters of angry women,
their impossible tits daring me to find the chopper hidden behind them.
The Formica counter, too, is peppered with crushed

Busch Light cans, and just beneath the smell of beer and shop grease
is the memory of tonic and shaving cream. High-and-tights
from my mother because she preferred her men squared away.

I see her always in parts, scattered through the rooms
of my life as I move through them. In a dusty half-shell helmet which lies,
butted in the corner. In how she kneed it's plastic dome

and her iced tea between her legs as we sat on the back steps
waiting for my father to return in his brown van from his ten-hour shift
at UPS before we rode the Honda, me clasped around her,

around Ray Fosse Park. And though it's no wonder her love
for two wheels and the lesser known roads has passed
to me, this antique Norton motorcycle sprawled around my feet—

its history skittered across the floor's black and white linoleum—
brings me back only to her dying. Emblem scabbed
onto the dented, cherry tank. Forks dismembered to calcified seals

and springs. The removed seat, too, exposes a wiring harness
like nerves along the spinal cord. All the screws—all the parts—
here, and because it's been only a month since the Goldwingers

and the entire Shawnee chapter of Women on Wheels
  attended her funeral, even the smallest piece of the assembly
is a vice clenched in my chest.

◆

  Mitch emerges from the back, sweeping aside
a blue beach towel nailed to the doorway's mantel like freezer flaps.
  He has a gleaming tray of ratchets, screwdrivers,

and stainless medical tools he bought at auction before the city
  tore the hospital down. Wears a white apron, clean,
and antiseptic of grease. He knows me, and he knows why

  I varnished the jets, revving the needle to redline
and dumping fuel in the oilcase. Shows me the operating table
  mounted on the pneumatic barber's stand,

how the foot pumps it. Tips my bike onto the burnished surface,
  and I'm by her side again reading the Velveteen Rabbit, tracing
her forehead's blue lines while she talks her little girl talk.

  Three years it took the doctors and the drugs to part her out,
to be released from her body's pieces. But Mitch knows also
  distraction's mercy—the salving effect of passing the tray—

describing for me the tools' shape and function as he calls for them.
  The way he pries the cover of the oilcase as if trepanning
an eggshell. Shaves with a scalpel's infinite precision

  bits of hardened gasket. Looking outside to a dog
huffing steam into the window, cigarette smoke screens my face
  and it's difficult to get a breath because no steady hands

could remove the black fluid from her lung's lobes and because
  the moment before she died I throttled from death's yeasty odor
lingering there at her bedroom's crystal doorknob,

  screaming at ninety and downshifting the last second
before cresting Norman Hill where anything above sixty sends you
  ass-over-teakettle into a cow pasture dotted with bales of hay.

I blink and something comes loose inside me, falls away
  like a plastic piece which has come off inside a broken toy.
Only now the toy works. The screen clears and I see he has

  reassembled the carburetor's jets and floats back into a chamber
of fire and air. With a hiss the table is lowered. He adds gas and oil,
  the manna of machinery. Mitch says I'll get him later,

claps me on the back as I wheel it into sunlight, the street outside.
  Someone waves, yells "Jonny boy!" and, rising into the light
I see is there, I thumb the ignition for every time

  she and I fired up together. For everything in that moment's
combustion of sound, everything whispered in exhaust.

HOW WE BURY OUR DEAD

Acknowledgements

I would like to extend my gratitude to the City of Murphysboro, and to my brothers at the Murphysboro Fire Department. Thank you also to my brothers from the 126th Air Refueling Wing Fire Department at Scott Air Force Base, O'Fallon, Illinois, the 156th CES Fire Department in Puerto Rico, the 151st Air Refueling Wing Fire Department in Salt Lake City, Utah, and the 179th Airlift Wing Fire Department in Mansfield, OH. Thank you also Alan Knabe, Horace Woods, Sean Fryman, and Thunder Heard.

A special thanks to longtime friend and mentor Judy Jordan, and also to Rodney Jones, Allison Joseph, Jon Tribble, and Andrew McSorley. Also to Steven Bryan Miller, Gordon Plumb, Rebecca St. John, Katie Ehlers, and to my father and friend, Van Travelstead, for much more than I have room to list.

Thank you also to Josh Ritter and Ruben Quesada, and also to Kevin Stein and all others involved with the Illinois Emerging Writers Program through Bradley University.

Thank you to Cobalt Press' Andrew Keating, as well as Stacie, Carlene, Tabitha and the editors of Cobalt Review.

And for Heidi Kristina Kocher, thank you.

Previous Publications and Awards

Poems and excerpts from this collection have appeared in *Prime Number, Uproot, The Baltimore Review, The Iowa Review, Dogwood Literary Review, Caesura, I-70 Review, Atticus Review, Tule Review, Reed Magazine, Sixfold, The Lindenwood Review, Sugared Water, Sierra Nevada Review, Verseweavers, The Poet's Billow, Aquillrelle, Trigger Happy: Poetry Saved My Life, TAB: The Journal of Poetry and Poetics, Proud to Be: Writing by American Warriors, Volume 2*, and *Cobalt Review.*

"Bazaar," "Hajji," and "Martinez" appeared in *Prime Number's Editors' Selections, Volume 4.*

"Bazaar" was nominated for a 2014 Pushcart Prize.

"Captain America. Ali Al Saleem Airbase, Kuwait" was a finalist for the 2014 Atlantis Award and nominated for a 2013 Pushcart Prize.

"Clam Gulch, Alaska" won the 2010 Roxana Rivera Memorial Poetry Contest, Southern Illinois University of Carbondale.

"DuPont Paint Factory" won the 2013 Gwendolyn Brooks Emerging Writers Competition, selected by Illinois Poet Laureate Kevin Stein.

"Mitch's Motorcycle Salvage and Rebuild". won the 2011 Roxana Rivera Memorial Poetry Contest, Southern Illinois University of Carbondale.

"Trucker" won the 2014 Cobalt Writing Prize for poetry.

"Still-life, Falling" placed third in the Oregon Poetry Association's Spring 2014 contest for experimental poetry.

About the Author

Jonathan Travelstead served in the Air Force National Guard for six years as a firefighter during which he did a tour in Kuwait during the Operation: Iraqi Freedom campaign, spending some time after in Alaska. Having since finished his MFA in Poetry at Southern Illinois University of Carbondale, he currently works as a full-time firefighter for a small town in the hills of Southern Illinois.

More Titles from Cobalt Press

Four Fathers: fiction and poetry ($15.00)
Dave Housley, BL Pawelek, Ben Tanzer, Tom Williams
Foreword by Greg Olear

Black Krim: a novella ($15.00)
Kate Wyer

Enter Your Initials for Record Keeping ($16.00)
Brian Oliu, featuring Player Two essays from Alissa Nutting, Sal Pane, Tyler Gobble, xTx, Josh McCall, Colin Rafferty, and others.
Forthcoming June 2015

A Horse Made of Fire: poetry ($14.00)
Heather Bell
Forthcoming August 2015

Cobalt Review, Volume 3: 2014 ($12.00)

Thumbnail Magazine 6 ($10.00)
Guest edited by Aubrey Hirsch

Additional 2015 titles to be announced.

For more information about Cobalt Press publications, including our quarterly and annual literary journals, visit:

cobaltreview.com/cobalt-press.

CPSIA information can be obtained
at www.ICGtesting.com
Printed in the USA
FFOW05n0127020315